United States
Department of
Agriculture

Forest Service

Pacific Northwest
Research Station

General Technical
Report
PNW-GTR-603
April 2004

Guide to the Common *Potentilla* Species of the Blue Mountains Ecoregion

Marti Aitken and
Catherine Gray Parks

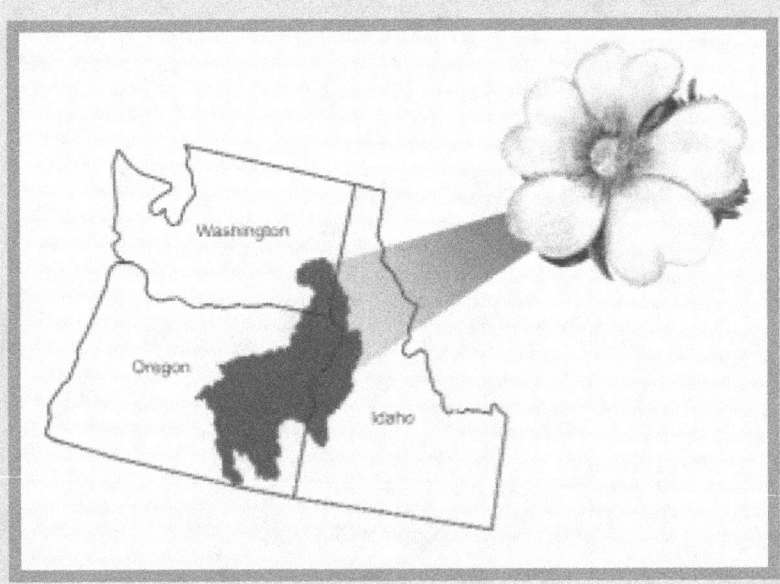

Authors
Marti Aitken is a botanist and geographer, and **Catherine Gray Parks** is a research plant pathologist, Forestry and Range Sciences Laboratory, 1401 Gekeler Lane, La Grande, OR 97850.

Guide to the Common *Potentilla* Species of the Blue Mountains Ecoregion

Marti Aitken and Catherine Gray Parks

U.S. Department of Agriculture, Forest Service
Pacific Northwest Research Station
Portland, Oregon
General Technical Report PNW-GTR-603
April 2004

Abstract

Aitken, Marti; Parks, Catherine Gray. 2004. Guide to the common *Potentilla* species of the Blue Mountains ecoregion. Gen. Tech. Rep. PNW-GTR-603. Portland, OR: U.S. Department of Agriculture, Forest Service, Pacific Northwest Research Station. 50 p.

This guide will assist field identification of *Potentilla* species likely to be found in the Blue Mountains region. Many species formerly classified in the genus *Potentilla* are also included. Illustrations accompany the descriptions and glossary.

Keywords: *Potentilla,* plant key, Blue Mountains.

Important Notes

The species included in this guide are based on a search of the U.S. Department of Agriculture (USDA) *Plants Database* (USDA NRCS 2002). Common taxa are represented, but this may not be a complete inventory. Many species formerly included in the genus *Potentilla* have been included. Nomenclature follows the *Plants Database* at the time of publication. Synonymy for species is provided in the species description.

This guide will help in the field identification of *Potentilla* species likely to be found throughout the Blue Mountains region, especially when flowers are not available. Many of the distinguishing features may require magnification to be seen. A 10X hand lens is usually sufficient. Unless otherwise noted, characteristics are based on mature structures (e.g., a mature leaf, not a newly emergent leaf). The genus *Potentilla* is well known for its difficulties in identification owing to hybridization and apomictic reproduction (seed production without fertilization) of some species. Determinations should always be confirmed by comparison with herbarium material and full descriptions, which can be found in the literature cited below.

This booklet consists of two main sections and an illustrated glossary. The first section is a dichotomous key with illustrations of identifying features. The illustrations are intended to highlight features of a particular species and to clarify terminology used in the key. No scale is implied. Illustration numbers correspond to leads in the key. The second section is organized alphabetically by taxa and consists of pictures, descriptions, and notes about each taxon. Most of the illustrations have been selected or modified from Hitchcock and Cronquist (1977) and from Harris and Harris (2001). Species descriptions are based primarily on Hitchcock and Cronquist (1977).

Acknowledgments

Specimens used to develop this key came from the Intermountain Herbarium, Eastern Oregon University Herbarium, Oregon State University Herbarium, and Wallowa-Whitman National Forest Herbarium. Stuart Markow, Leila Shultz, Jean Wood, and Gene Yates provided helpful comments on the manuscript.

English Equivalents

1 millimeter (mm) = 0.0394 inch
1 centimeter (cm) = 0.394 inch
1 decimeter (dm) = 3.94 inch
1 meter (m) = 3.28 feet

References

Harris, J.G.; Harris, M.E. 2001. Plant identification terminology: an illustrated guide. Payson, UT: Spring Lake Publishing. 206 p.

Hitchcock, C.L.; Cronquist, A. 1977. Part 3: Saxifragaceae to Ericaceae. In: Flora of the Pacific Northwest. 3[d] ed. Seattle, WA: University of Washington Press: 126-157.

Hitchcock, C.L.; Cronquist, A. 1998. Flora of the Pacific Northwest: an illustrated manual. 11th ed. Seattle, WA: University of Washington Press. 730 p.

U.S. Department of Agriculture, Natural Resources Conservation Service [USDA NRCS]. 2002. The plants database, version 3.5. Baton Rouge, LA: National Plant Data Center. http://plants.usda.gov. (10 December 2003).

Potentilla

The Blue Mountains ecoregion as used in this guide includes Baker, Crook, Grant, Harney, Malheur, Morrow, Umatilla, Union, Wallowa, and Wheeler Counties in Oregon as well as Asotin, Columbia, Garfield, and Walla Walla Counties in Washington. The region encompasses several mountain ranges including the Strawberry, Greenhorn, Elkhorn, Aldrich, and Maury Ranges as well as the Blue, Ochoco, and Wallowa Mountains. Ecosystems in the region include ponderosa shrub forests, western ponderosa forests, Douglas-fir forests, grand fir-Douglas-fir forests, western spruce-fir forests, juniper steppe woodland, mountain mahogany-oak scrub, Great Basin sagebrush, wheatgrass-bluegrass, alpine meadows and barrens, and sagebrush steppe. Among the plants of the Blue Mountains forests and grasslands are *Potentilla,* ancient members of the rose family that have evolved to survive the elevation, moisture, and temperature extremes of this region.

Most of the 23 *Potentilla* (or former *Potentilla*) species in the Blue Mountains ecoregion are annual, biennial, or perennial herbs. The one exception is the shrub *Dasiphora floribunda,* a former *Potentilla* species. Typically the *Potentilla* species in this area have a scaly caudex, a taproot, and well-developed, pinnately or digitately compound leaves. The margins of the leaflets are serrate, toothed, or dissected, but rarely entire.

The inflorescences are usually cymose or rarely of solitary axillary flowers. Each flower consists of three whorls of nonreproductive structures (bractlets, sepals, and petals), which are fused at the base into a disk- or cup-shaped extension of the floral axis (fig. 1). Five bractlets form the outermost whorl. The middle whorl consists of five sepals that are usually larger than the bractlets. The innermost whorl consists of five deciduous petals that are most often yellow, but sometimes white. Petal shape varies from obovate to almost circular, or notched at the apex. A disk usually lines the fused structure.

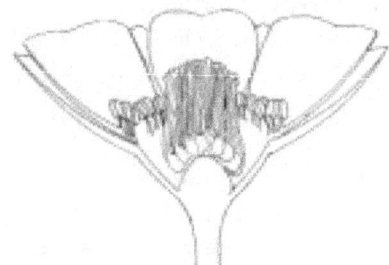

Figure 1–Cross section of *Potentilla* flower.

3

The flowers have both male (stamens) and female (pistils) reproductive organs. Stamens usually number 20, but may be as few as 10 or as many as 30. Usually, the stamens are arranged in three whorls with the 5 largest directly opposite the sepals, 5 directly opposite the petals, and 10 arranged toward the edges of the petals. The anthers are basally attached to the filaments. At maturity, the anthers split open along the sides, open widely, and release the pollen. The pistils are more numerous (usually more than 10) and are attached on a conical or hemispherical receptacle. The style is deciduous and may be attached terminally, laterally, or basally. The fruit consists of numerous, smooth to wrinkled or net-veined achenes.

Collectively, members of *Potentilla* are commonly referred to as "cinquefoils." Cinquefoil gets its name from an old French word meaning "five-leaf." The Latin name *Potentilla* refers to the medicinal potency of the herb. Cinquefoil's medicinal value was recognized by a Greek naturalist and student of Aristotle, Theophrastus, who was the first to describe it and claimed its ability to cure fevers and diarrhea. Also, cinquefoil was reputedly an ingredient in many spells in the Middle Ages, and reportedly was used also in love divinations. It was one of the ingredients of a special bait for fishing nets that would ensure a large catch.

Little is known of the role that *Potentilla* performs in the complex ecology of the Blue Mountains, although many members of the rose family are noted as important food sources for wildlife. One species of particular interest is *Potentilla recta* (page 41). A native of Eurasia, *Potentilla recta* (sulfur cinquefoil) is found in central and southern Europe, the Middle East, the mountains of north Africa, and western and central Asia. *Potentilla recta* was introduced to North America prior to 1900. In eastern North America, *P. recta* is considered to be primarily a minor agricultural weed. However, in the last two decades, *P. recta* has been recognized as having a broad ecological amplitude in the drier climates of northwestern North America where it forms dense populations and is considered a threat to native plant communities.

Infestations of *P. recta* have been detected in several locations in the Blue Mountains. Roadsides, waste places, abandoned agriculture fields, clearcuts, and other disturbed sites are particularly susceptible to invasion by *P. recta*, but some low-disturbance sites also are susceptible, including native bunchgrass communities, and interior mixed-conifer forests. It can pose a serious management threat in many natural areas owing to its prolific seeding ability. When plant communities become thoroughly infested by *P. recta,* native plant biodiversity decreases and natural successional processes become altered. Of particular concern is the risk that *P. recta* may pose to reproductive success of the many native cinquefoils that are frequently found to co-occur with *P. recta* at mid-elevations.

Control of this invasive nonnative plant is hindered because it often is confused with native cinquefoils that are found in the Northwest. *Potentilla recta* has three unique characteristics: (1) long, right-angled hairs perpendicular to the leafstalks and stem, (2) numerous stem leaves but few basal leaves, and (3) a netlike pattern on the seed coat. Although varietal treatments exceed the scope of this publication, we have included varieties of *P. gracilis* because of the similarities to *P. recta.*

Plant Key

1a Plants shrubby and stems woody ....*Dasiphora floribunda*
1b Plants generally herbaceous (may be somewhat woody at base) 2

2a Leaves pinnate ....4, GROUP I
2b Leaves digitate, subdigitate, or ternate...3

2a   2b

Harris and Harris (2001)

3a Basal leaves with 3 leaflets ....14, GROUP II
3b Basal leaves with at least 5 leaflets.............................20, GROUP III

GROUP I: Leaves pinnate

4a Plants spreading by long, freely rooting stolons (strawberry-like),
     or by rhizomes 5
4b Plants from rootstock or other and not spreading by stolons or
     rhizomes 6

5a Plants spreading by rhizomes and rooting at the nodes; stems
     reddish; leaves light green; lower surface of leaves paler, glaucous,
     and variously pubescent; leaflets 5-7; flowers red to purple
     ....*Comarum palustre*
5b Plants spreading by stolons, not rooting at the nodes; stems and
     leaves generally silvery gray with spreading silky hairs; upper leaf
     surface grayish to green, lower leaf surface whitish; leaflets 15-25;
     flowers yellow ....*Argentina anserina*

6a Leaves and forestem glandular, or with glandular hairs (may only be
     visible with magnification)...7

6b Leaves and forestem not glandular; hairs, if present,
not glandular 9

6a

Harris and Harris (2001)

7a Leaflets 3-5 (rarely 7), each 6-10 mm long and congested so that,
when laid flat, the leaflets overlap; basal leaf petioles usually much
longer than the blade ....*P. brevifolia*
7b Leaflets 5-11, each 1-4 cm long and not congested, although
leaflets may be crowded together; petiole usually shorter than
the blade 8

7a   7b

Hitchcock and Cronquist (1977)

8a Mature plants mostly >4 dm tall; stems very pilose, or villous,
often with multicelled, moniliform, brownish hairs that may give
the stem a dirty appearance, especially near the top; leaves sometimes almost hairless to very hirsute; leaflets 5-11; inflorescence
narrow and erect; sepals mostly 6-8 mm; petals usually as long as
or longer than the sepals.......................................*P. arguta*
8b Mature plants mostly <4 dm; stems may be hairless to densely
pilose-glandular; leaves sometimes hairless, glandular-pubescent to
short-hirsute and only weakly glandular; leaflets 5-9; inflorescence
open; sepals <6 mm long; petals sometimes shorter than the sepals
....*P. glandulosa*

8a   8b

Hitchcock and Cronquist (1977)

9a   Leaflets numerous (7-21), usually crowded along rachis, and
     pinnately dissected into small (usually <1 cm long) segments;
     plants prostrate, decumbent, or ascending 10
9b   Leaflets few (5-13), and deeply cleft, but neither dissected into
     small segments nor crowded; plants upright and generally erect ...11

10a Leaves mostly cauline, few basal; leaflets 7-15, each 3-5 mm
     long, divided nearly to midrib into 3-7 unequal linear to
     elliptic segments; plants of dry lakeshores and vernal pools
     ....*P. newberryi*
10b Leaves mostly basal; leaflets 9-21, each 5-12 mm long, pedately
     divided nearly to base into 3-5 (rarely 7) linear segments; plants
     of moist meadows to open ridges and barren slopes.............*P. ovina*

10a   10b

Hitchcock and Cronquist (1977)

11a Leaflets toothed, but not deeply cleft; plant from a simple
     taproot..*P. paradoxa*

8

11b Leaflets deeply cleft, often more than halfway to midvein; plant
from a branched, often woody, caudex...12

11a   12a

Hitchcock and Cronquist (1977)

12a Leaves greenish on both surfaces, variously pubescent; leaflets
obovate-cuneate, the upper three often confluent; leaflet
margins cleft about halfway to midvein into linear or
lanceolate teeth ....*P. drummondii*
12b Leaves grayish throughout or greenish on upper surface and
white on lower surface, very pubescent; leaflets oblong,
oblong-lanceolate, or oblanceolate, upper three not confluent.....13

13a Leaflets 5-9, irregularly lobed ½ to ⅔ of the distance to midrib
into linear, forward-pointing segments; lower leaflets often
reduced and upper three largest; upper surfaces of leaves usually
greenish, lower surfaces usually whitish ....*P. pensylvanica*
13b Leaflets sharply lanceolately toothed to midvein; upper and lower
leaflets similarly sized; upper surfaces of leaves greenish or grayish,
lower surfaces usually grayish...*P. hippiana*

13a   13b

Hitchcock and Cronquist (1977)

GROUP II: Basal leaves with 3 leaflets

14a Stems single, arising from a single taproot; plants generally tall
(1-6 dm), and in moist meadows, along stream or pond banks,
or in waste areas 15

14b Stems single, or multiple arising from a branched, often woody,
base; low plants (<3 dm) usually of alpine environments 17

15a Pubescence on lower surfaces of leaflets with a mixture of fine,
spreading hairs and thicker (often darker) glandular hairs; upper
surface with short stiff hairs....................................... *P. biennis*

15b Pubescence on lower leaf surfaces not a mixture of fine and thick
hairs, and not glandular; pubescence on upper surface various,
but not of short stiff hairs. 16

| 15a | 16a | 16b |

Hitchcock and Cronquist (1977)

16a Lower surface of leaflets with coarse, stiff hairs; and upper surfaces
with somewhat short, soft, woolly hairs; larger hairs often with
small blisters at the base ....*P. norvegica*

16b Lower and upper surfaces of leaflets densely covered with fine
hairs, spreading or pressed flat against the surface areas........*P. rivalis*

17a Leaves equally or almost equally green on both surfaces,
puberulent or with irregularly curled or crooked hairs (especially
on upper plant); petioles usually 2 to 3 times as long as blade;
plant 15-25 cm tall...*P. flabellifolia*

17b Lower surface of leaf, and/or upper surface of leaf grayish, or the under surface covered with either whitish, short, soft woolly hairs, or dense, long silky hairs; petioles rarely more than twice as long as blade; plant usually ≤15 cm tall 18

17a   18a

Hitchcock and Cronquist (1977)

18a Stems, calyx, and lower surface of leaves usually woolly; leaflets leathery, dark grayish-green above and prominently veined beneath, the surface covered with short, soft woolly hairs ....*P. villosa*

18b Stems, calyx, and lower surface of leaves variously pubescent, and if woolly, then leaflets not leathery and not prominently veined beneath 19

19a   19b

Hitchcock and Cronquist (1977)

19a Petioles and lower stem tomentose; upper surface of leaves often strigose; leaflets 5-15 mm, oblong-obovate to more or less oval ....*P. nivea*

19b Petioles and lower stem pilose; upper surface of leaves hirsute; leaflets 10-20 mm, cuneate-obovate to obovate-rhombic ......*P. uniflora*

GROUP III: Basal leaves with at least 5 leaflets

20a Leaves minutely glandular or glandular pubescent 21
20b Leaves variously pubescent, but not glandular or glandular
pubescent...22

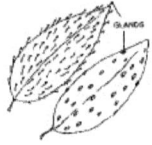

20a
Harris and Harris (2001)

21a Leaflets toothed less than halfway to midvein; lower surface of
leaves densely white-tomentose ....*P. pulcherrima*
21b Leaflets toothed at least halfway to the midvein; both leaf surfaces
greenish and hirsute ....*P. gracilis* var. *brunnescens*

21a   21b

Hitchcock and Cronquist (1977)

22a Leaves mostly cauline...23
22b Leaves mostly basal 24

23a Leaves mostly oriented upright; leaf surfaces more or less equally
green; leaflets 5-7, each 3-7 cm, often folded along the prominent
midveins; leaflet margins serrate-lobate with divergent, forward-
pointing teeth extending about halfway to midvein, not revolute;
pubescence on leaves and stems stiff, spreading nearly
perpendicular to surface, and often somewhat sparkly; length
of stem hairs almost equal to stem width ....*P. recta*

23b Leaf orientation various, but seldom upright; leaf surfaces often green above, gray below; leaflets 5, each 1-2 cm long, generally flat; leaflet margins lobate-serrate ½ to ¾ of the way to midvein into narrowly oblong segments; leaflet margins often revolute; pubescence both tomentum and silky to stiff hairs, longest hairs not equaling stem width ....*P. argentea*

23a   23b

Hitchcock and Cronquist (1977)

24a Plant a tall (1-4 dm) somewhat rangy annual or biennial.....*P. rivalis*
24b Plant size various, but always perennial 25

25a Leaflets 5-7, each 1-3 cm; plant up to 4.5 dm tall 26
25b Leaflets 7-9, each 3-8 cm; plants 4-8 dm tall 27

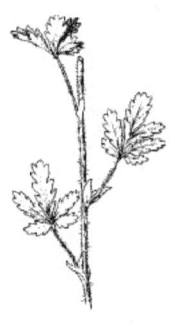

24a   26a   26b

Hitchcock and Cronquist (1977)

26a Plants 15-45 cm tall; lower surface of leaflets sparsely
hirsute-strigose and greenish, to grayish sericeous; leaflet
margins triangularly toothed to dissected (almost to midvein)
....*P. diversifolia*

26b Plants up to 6 cm tall; lower surface of leaflets whitish-tomentose
and usually also strongly strigose-hirsute (to sericeous); leaflet
margins from deeply cleft into linear segments to shallowly
few-toothed at the tip ....*P. concinna*

27a Leaflets dissected ⅔ of the way to midvein into linear segments;
leaf undersurface grayish and hairy 28

27b Leaflets dissected less than ⅔ of the way to midvein into
lanceolate lobes, leaf undersurface greenish 29

28a Leaflets greenish above, white-tomentose beneath; margins often
revolute ....*P. gracilis* var. *flabelliformis*

28b Leaflets grayish above, silky to tomentose beneath; margins not
revolute ....*P. pectinisecta*

28a   28b

Hitchcock and Cronquist (1977)

29a Leaflets often greenish and equally pubescent above and beneath
....*P. gracilis* var. *fastigiata*

29b Leaflets variously colored, but not equally pubescent above and
beneath 30

30a Leaflets rounded at the tip; margins rarely cleft halfway to midvein ....*P. pulcherrima*

30b Leaflets apex blunt or obtuse; leaflet margins mostly cleft halfway to midvein...*P. gracilis* var. *gracilis*

30a   30b

Hitchcock and Cronquist (1977)

Silverweed cinquefoil   *Argentina anserina* (L.) Rydb.

Description: Grayish, strongly stoloniferous perennial.
Height: Prostrate.
Leaves: Whitish-silky-woolly on both sides to greenish above; 1-3 dm
    long, pinnate; leaflets 15-25, obovate to oblong, rounded, sharply and
    coarsely serrate, 1-3.5 cm.
Pubescence: Glabrous on lower parts of plant, but becoming more or
    less hairy and purplish-glandular above.
Flowers: Solitary at the stolon nodes; calyx silky; sepals ovate-triangular,
    4-6 mm; petals yellow and rounded, 8-12 mm; May-Aug.
Habitat: Meadows, streambanks, and pond margins.
Notes: Native; spreads by long freely rooting stolons; leaf pubescence is
    highly variable. This is an obiligate wetland species in Idaho, Oregon,
    and Washington.
Synonymy: *Argentina anserina* (L.) Rydb. var. *concolor* (Ser.) Rydb.;
    A. argentea (L.) Rydb.; *Potentilla anserina* L.; *P. anserina* L. var.
    concolor Ser.; *P. anserina* L. var. *sericea* Hayne; *P. anserina* L. var.
    yukonensis (Hultén) Boivin; *P. egedii* Wormsk. ssp. *yukonensis* (Hultén)
    Hultén; *P. yukonensis* Hultén.

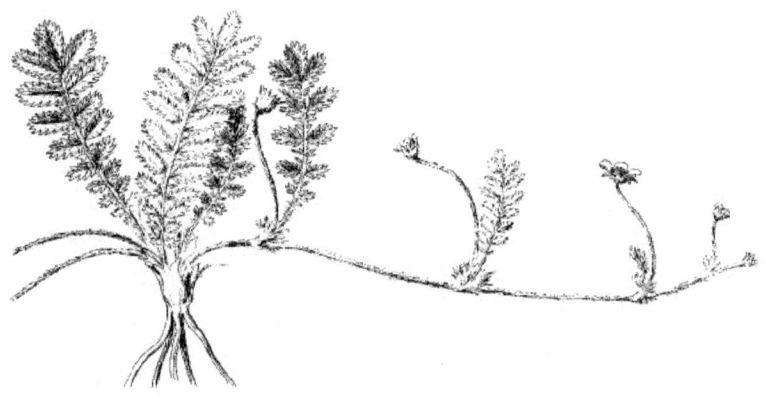

Modified from Hitchcock and Cronquist (1977)

Purple marshlocks   *Comarum palustre* L.

Description: Strongly rhizomatous perennial with reddish stems up to
  1 m long.
Height: Floating or prostrate.
Leaves: Pinnate, 5-7 leaflets, glabrous to sparsely strigose; upper surface
  light green; lower surface paler, glaucous, and with sparsely to
  copiously whitish-strigose to appressed silky pubescence; leaflets 3-6 cm,
  obovate to oblong or narrowly elliptic-oblong; leaflet margins shallowly
  crenate-serrate to deeply serrate.
Pubescence: Glabrous on lower parts of plant, but becoming more or
  less hairy and purplish-glandular above.
Flowers: Deep red to purple, usually numerous in open, one-sided
  cymes; June-Aug.
Habitat: Wet areas such as bogs, meadows, creek banks, and lake
  margins, from sea level to subalpine areas.
Notes: Native. This is an obligate wetland species in Idaho, Oregon, and
  Washington. Although substantial variation occurs, geographic races
  have not been differentiated.
Synonymy: *Potentilla palustris* (L.) Scop.; *P. palustris* (L.) Scop. var.
  parvifolia (Raf.) Fern. & Long; *P. palustris* (L.) Scop. var. *villosa*
  (Pers.) Lehm.

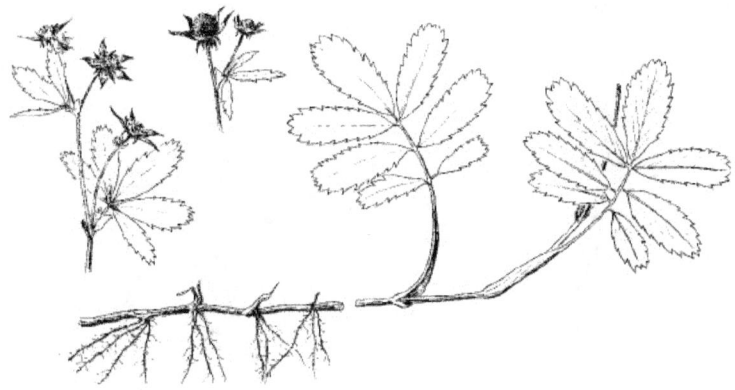

Modified from Hitchcock and Cronquist (1977)

17

Shrubby cinquefoil   *Dasiphora floribunda* (Pursh)
                                          Kartesz, comb. nov. ined.

Description: Spreading to erect grayish shrub, with reddish-brown, shredding bark.

Height: 1-10 (16) dm tall.

Leaves: Pinnately 5 (sometimes 3 or 7) foliate; leaflets crowded, 10-20 mm long, linear to narrowly elliptic-oblong, entire, often revolute margined; appressed silky and more or less grayish, especially on lower surface of leaves.

Pubescence: New growth silky-pilose, becoming glabrate with maturity.

Flowers: Either single in leaf axils or in small open terminal cymes with 3-7 flowers; petals yellow, oval to ovate-oblong 8-13 mm. June-Aug.

Habitat: Lower foothills to subalpine slopes.

Notes: Native. Now recognized as member of the genus *Dasiphora*, it is still widely referred to as a *Potentilla* and has been included in this treatment for that reason. This species is a facultative wetland species in Idaho, Oregon, and Washington. Numerous horticultural variants exist.

Synonyms: *Dasiphora fruticosa* auct. non (L.) Rydb.; *Pentaphylloides floribunda* (Pursh) A. Löve nom. super.; *Pentaphylloides fruticosa* auct. non (L.) O. Schwarz; *Potentilla floribunda* Pursh; *P. fruticosa* auct. non L.; *P. fruitcosa* L. ssp. *floribunda* (Pursh) Elkington; *P. fruitcosa* L. var. *tenuifolia* Lehm.

Modified from Hitchcock and Cronquist (1977)

Silver cinquefoil

Potentilla argentea L.

Description: Grayish perennial from woody caudex.

Height: (1) 1.5-3 (5) dm.

Leaves: Mainly cauline; 5 oblanceolate, digitate leaflets with lobate-serrate margins extending ½ to ¾ of the way to the midvein, and more or less revolutely margined teeth.

Pubescence: Mixture of tomentum and silky to stiff hairs.

Flowers: Yellow, obovate-cuneate petals, rounded to somewhat notched at the apex; equaling or slightly exceeding the sepals; sepals 2-3 mm; June-July.

Habitat: Scattered localities including ponderosa pine forests and gravelly river banks.

Notes: Introduced from Europe. Similar to *P. recta* in presence of cauline leaves, but herbage is grayish and usually tomentose. *P. argentea* is typically a smaller plant.

Synonymy: None.

Hitchcock and Cronquist (1977)

19

Tall cinquefoil   *Potentilla arguta* **Pursh**

Description: Tall perennial, often reddish, and glandular-puberulent.

Height: (3) 4-8 (10) dm

Leaves: Mostly basal; may be glabrate to short-hirsute and glandular-pubescent; pinnate with 7-9 ovate elliptic 1.5-4 cm leaflets; leaflet margins deeply dentate-serrate to doubly dentate or incised.

Pubescence: Stems strongly pilose or villous with multicellular moniliform glandular, brownish hairs; leaves, short-hirsute to glandular-puberulent to hairless.

Flowers: Inflorescence narrow; petals range from creamy-white to yellow, and may be subequal to or up to 2 mm longer than the large (6-8 mm) sepals; May-July.

Habitat: Widespread.

Notes: This species can sometimes be indistinguishable from *P. glandulosa.* Generally, the tall growth habit and the narrow inflorescence with large sepals, make this species fairly distinctive. There are two varieties: *convallaria,* which occurs throughout the tri-state area, and *arguta,* which occurs in Idaho.

Synonymy: None.

Tall cinquefoil   *Potentilla arguta* Pursh

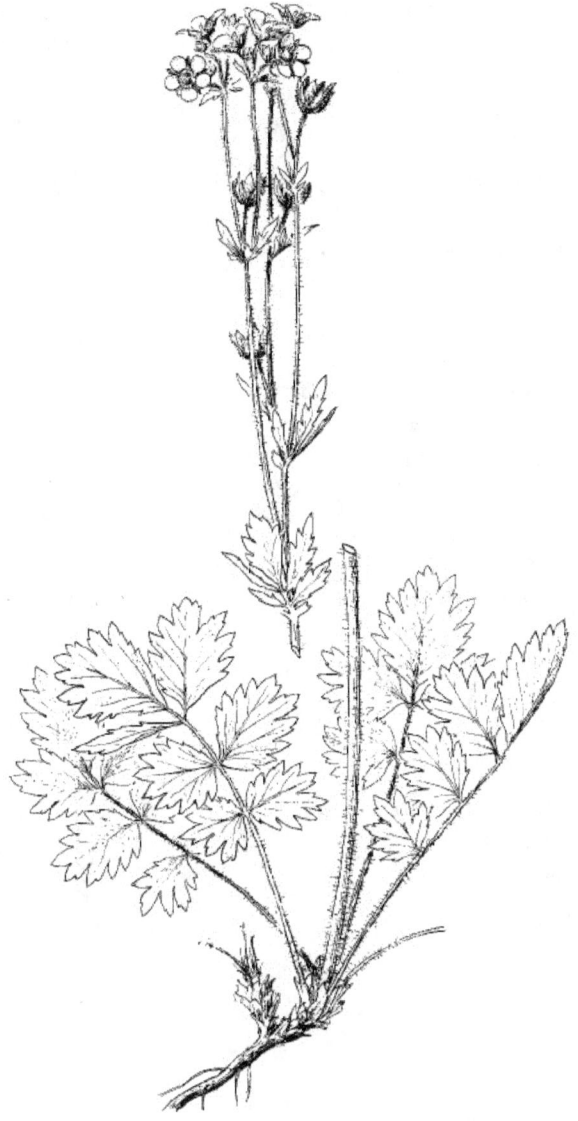

Hitchcock and Cronquist (1977)

Biennial cinquefoil

Description: Annual or biennial from a slender taproot and a simple branched caudex.

Height: 1-6 dm.

Leaves: Mostly cauline and reduced upward; ternate (although sometimes 4 or 5 leaflets), obovate to oblanceolate, coarsely crenate-serrate, 1-4 cm.

Pubescence: Mixture of fine, slender, spreading to somewhat tomentose hairs and thicker, multicellular, glandular hairs.

Flowers: Glandular-puberulent; sepals erect, ovate triangular; petals yellow, cuneate-obovate and about half the sepal length; May-Aug.

Habitat: Disturbed areas such as roadsides. Also in moist sandy sites and in moist meadows.

Notes: Native. *P. biennis* is a facultative wetland species in this region.

Synonymy: None.

Potentilla biennis Greene

Hitchcock and Cronquist (1977)

Sparseleaf cinquefoil

Potentilla brevifolia Nutt. ex
Torr. & Gray

Description: Short, yellowish-green perennial with few leaves, and
forming mats up to 20 cm in diameter.

Height: Up to 20 cm.

Leaves: Mostly basal, pinnate; petiole usually much longer than the
blade; leaflets 5 (sometimes 3 or 7), crowded, each 6-10 mm, generally
orbicular, crenate, and shallowly incised 1 or 2 times.

Pubescence: Finely glandular-puberulent, often glabrous but occasionally
sparsely pilose near top of plant.

Flowers: Numerous open, branched cymes; sepals 3-5 mm oval to
oblong-lanceolate, spreading to slightly ascending; petals yellow,
broadly obovate and spreading, 2-3 mm longer than sepals; July-Aug.

Habitat: High mountains.

Notes: Native.

Synonymy: None.

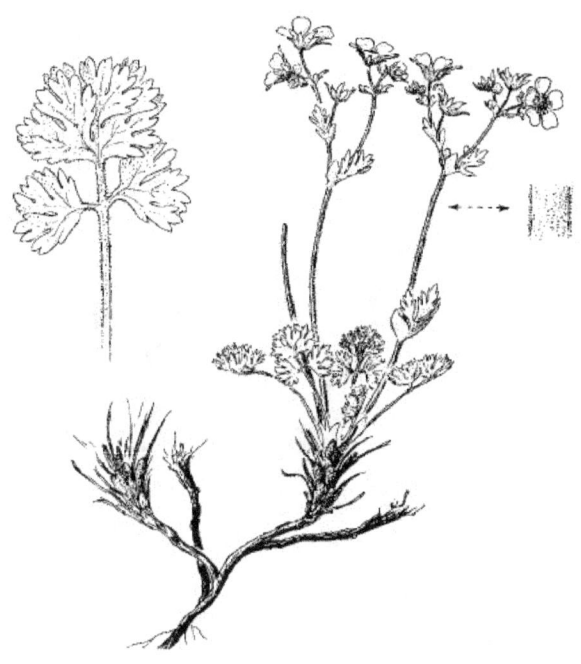

Hitchcock and Cronquist (1977)

Elegant cinquefoil   *Potentilla concinna* **Richards.**

Description: Low, spreading to ascending, grayish to greenish perennial
  from a strongly taprooted, slightly branched caudex.
Height: Up to 6 cm; usually much broader than tall.
Leaves: Mostly digitate or subdigitate with 5 to 7 leaflets, 1-3 cm; lower
  surface of leaves whitish-tomentose and often strongly strigose-hirsute;
  upper surface tomentose and sericeous or hirsute, to merely strigose or
  hirsute and grayish to pale green; leaflet margins from deeply cleft into
  linear segments to shallowly few-toothed at the tip.
Pubescence: Copiously hirsute-strigose and more or less grayish, to
  sparsely strigose and greenish.
Flowers: Small cymes of 3-7 flowers; sepals sericeous-villous and
  lanceolate, 3-6 mm; petals yellow, obovate, 6-9 mm; May-July.
Habitat: Sandy prairies and foothills to alpine ridges.
Notes: Native. Several intergradient varieties. Primarily in Idaho portion
  of the Blue Mountains region.
Synonymy: None at species level.

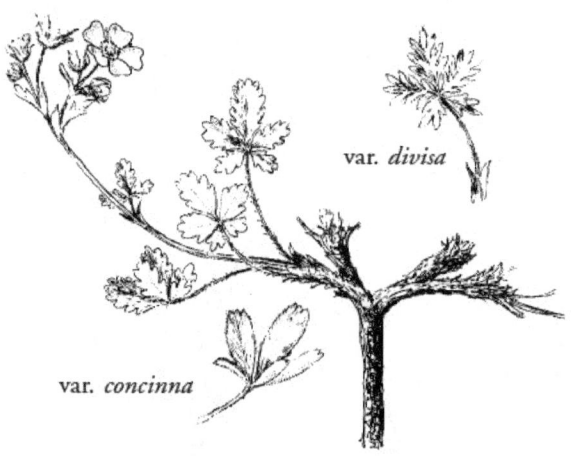

var. *divisa*

var. *concinna*

Hitchcock and Cronquist (1977)

Varileaf cinquefoil

Description: Greenish to grayish
perennial with branching
caudex and short thick
rootstocks.

Height: 1.5-4.5 dm.

Leaves: Mostly basal; digitate to
subdigitate; leaflets 5-7,
oblanceolate to broadly obovate,
1-3 cm, margins shallowly
triangular-toothed to
dissected into linear segments.

Pubescence: Varies from sparsely
hirsute-strigose and greenish to
grayish sericeous.

Flowers: Open cymes with many
yellow flowers; sepals
triangular-lanceolate, 4-6 mm;
petals obcordate, 6-9 mm.

Habitat: Streambanks in montane
to subalpine habitats; alpine
meadows, ledges and rocky slopes.

Notes: Native. May be confused
with *P. concinna*, but lacks
tomentose pubescence on leaf
undersurface. As the name
suggests, this species is
highly variable, especially in
leaf characteristics. Two
varieties, *perdissecta* and
diversifolia may occur in the
Blue Mountains region.
For a discussion of the variability
and treatment of the varieties,
see Hitchcock and Cronquist
(1977, 1998).

Synonymy: None at species level.

Potentilla diversifolia **Lehm.**

var. *perdissecta*

var. *diversifolia*

Hitchcock and Cronquist (1977)

Drummond's cinquefoil

Potentilla drummondii **Lehm.**

Description: Greenish perennial with branching crown and short, thick rootstocks.

Height: 2.5-4.5 dm.

Leaves: Pinnate; leaflets 5-9 (sometimes 11) closely crowded, obovate-cuneate, 2-5 cm, with the upper ones often confluent; leaflet margins cleft about halfway to midvein into linear or lanceolate teeth.

Pubescence: From slightly to copiously hirsute-strigose, but always greenish; often glabrate.

Flowers: Open, many-flowered cymes; sepals ovate, sparingly hirsute; petals yellow, obovate, to obcordate 6-11 mm; June-Aug.

Habitat: Subalpine to alpine wet meadows and open slopes.

Notes: Native. It is thought to be sympatric with and transitional to both *P. breweri* and *P. ovina* in southeast Oregon (Hitchcock and Cronquist 1977).

Synonymy: None.

Hitchcock and Cronquist (1977)

High mountain cinquefoil   *Potentilla flabellifolia*
                              Hook. ex Torr. & Gray

Description: Greenish perennial with branched crown, forming large clumps.

Height: 1.5-2.5 dm.

Leaves: Mainly basal with very long petioles; ternate; leaftlets cuneate-obovate to flabelliform, 1.5-2.5 cm; leaflet margins deeply crenate-dentate and often secondarily toothed.

Pubescence: Subglabrous to moderately puberulent or with irregularly curled, crooked hairs on upper plant.

Flowers: Few-flowered cymes; sepals deltoid-lanceolate; petals yellow, obcordate, up to 10 mm; June-Aug.

Habitat: Wet meadows and streambanks to alpine or subalpine ridges and talus slopes.

Notes: Native.

Synonymy: None.

Hitchcock and Cronquist (1977)

Sticky cinquefoil   *Potentilla glandulosa* **Lindl.**

Description: A highly variable perennial that is often somewhat sticky to touch.

Height: 1.5-4 (7) dm.

Leaves: Basal; pinnate, 5-9 leaflets; leaflets flabellate-cuneate to rhombic, obovate or oblong 1-3 cm, 1 or 2 times sharply serrate.

Pubescence: On stems varies from glabrous on lower plant to glandular-puberulent and hirsute to densely piloseglandular throughout; on leaves varies from hairless to short-hirsute to glandular pubescent; hairs from 1-celled to moniliform.

Flowers: Few-flowered, cyme; petals vary from dark to pale yellow (almost white), generally shorter to somewhat longer than sepals; May-July.

Habitat: Common.

Notes: Native. This species is highly variable and has numerous intergradient geographical races. Treatment of these races exceeds the scope of this publication, but can be found in Hitchcock and Cronquist (1977, 1998). The most common subspecies for this area are *glabrata* (formerly var. *intermedia*), *glandulosa, nevadensis,* and *pseudorupestris.* In addition, *P. glandulosa* is easily confused with *P. arguta.* It is most easily distinguished by its relatively open inflorescence and generally smaller size.

Synonymy: None at the species level.

Sticky cinquefoil   *Potentilla glandulosa* Lindl.

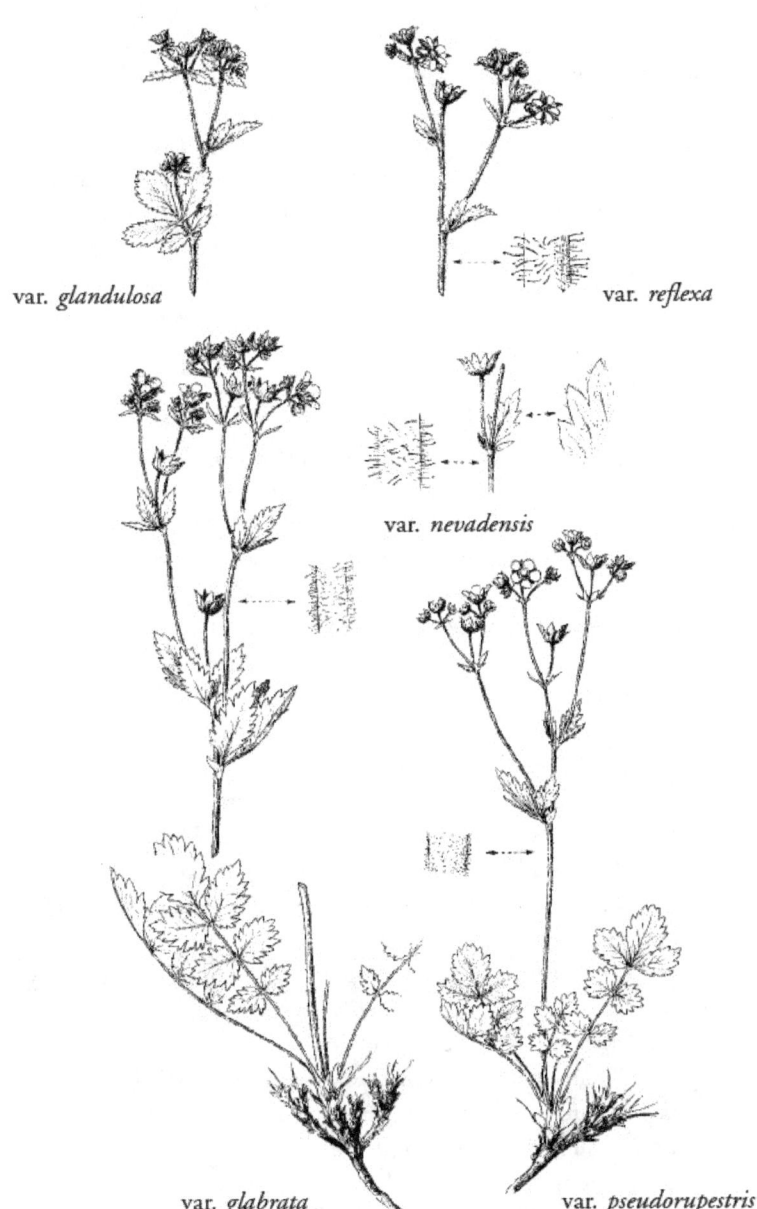

var. *glandulosa*

var. *reflexa*

var. *nevadensis*

var. *glabrata*

var. *pseudorupestris*

Hitchcock and Cronquist (1977)

Slender cinquefoil   *Potentilla gracilis*
                                          Dougl. ex Hook.

Description: Highly variable, erect to ascending perennial with a thick, branched caudex.

Height: 4-8 dm.

Leaves: Basal, numerous; digitate; glabrous or puberulent, sometimes glandular (var. *brunnescens*); leaflets 7-9, cuneate-oblanceolate to broadly oblanceolate or oblong-elliptic, usually 3-8 cm long (sometimes 2-12); leaflet margins crenate-dentate to very deeply dissected.

Pubescence: Usually strigose or minutely strigose, but varies from spreading-hirsute to puberulent to woolly.

Flowers: Open, many flowered cyme; sepals broadly lanceolate 4-7 mm, often glandular; petals yellow, obcordate 6-10 mm; June-Aug.

Habitat: Dry to moist meadows, grasslands, rocky slopes, open forests.

Notes: Native. The species is highly variable and taxonomic treatment is difficult. The four varieties that occur in the Blue Mountains are identified in the illustration. *Potentilla gracilis* may be confused with other species such as *P. pectinisecta, P. pulcherrima,* and *P. recta.* Both *P. pectinisecta* and *P. pulcherrima* were once treated as varieties of *P. gracilis. Potentilla pectinisecta* has leaflets lobed at least ⅔ of the way to the midvein, like *P. gracilis* var. *flabelliformis.* However, the leaf undersurface of *P. gracilis* var. *flabelliformis* is white-tomentose below and the upper surface is green, whereas the undersurface of *P. pectinisecta* is silky to tomentose, and the upper surface is grayish sericeous. *Potentilla pulcherrima* is also white-tomentose on the leaf undersurfaces, with teeth extending ⅙ to ⅔ of the way to the midvein. *Potentilla recta* has numerous cauline leaves, and the pubescence is at nearly right angles to the surface.

Synonymy: At the species level, there are none. Synonymy occurs only at varietal level. Synonyms for *Potentilla gracilis* Dougl. ex Hook. var. *fastigiata* (Nutt.) S. Wats. are as follows:

> *P. gracilis* Dougl. ex Hook. var. *blasckeana* (Turcz. ex Lehm.) Jepson; *P. gracilis* Dougl. ex Hook. var. *glabrata* (Lehm.) C.L. Hitchc.; *P. gracilis* Dougl. ex Hook. ssp. *nuttallii* (Lehm.) Keck; *P. gracilis* Dougl. ex Hook. var. *nuttallii* (Lehm.) Sheldon; *P. gracilis* Dougl. ex Hook. var. *permollis* (Rydb.) C.L. Hitchc.; *P. gracilis* Dougl. ex Hook. var. *rigida* S. Wats.

Slender cinquefoil

Potentilla gracilis
Dougl. ex Hook.

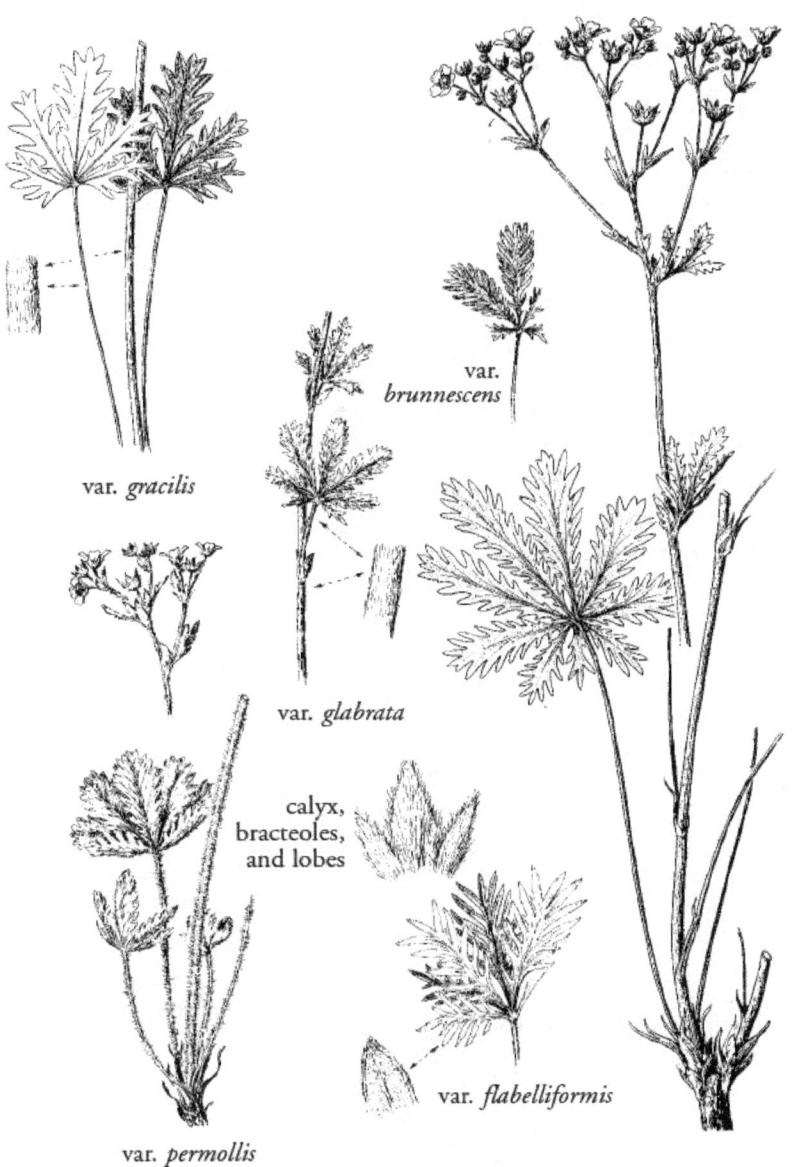

var. *gracilis*

var.
brunnescens

var. *glabrata*

calyx,
bracteoles,
and lobes

var. *flabelliformis*

var. *permollis*

Hitchcock and Cronquist (1977)

31

Potentilla hippiana Lehm.

Woolly cinquefoil

Description: Freely branched perennial with heavily branched crown, and a generally grayish appearance (upper leaf surfaces may be green).
Height: 2-5 dm.
Leaves: Grayish below, grayish or greenish above; pinnate; leaflets 7-11, crowded, oblong or oblong-oblanceolate, 2-5 cm; leaflet margins sharply lanceolate-toothed up to halfway to midvein.
Pubescence: Grayish-hirsute and tomentose throughout, eglandular.
Flowers: Freely branching cyme with ascending branches; sepals grayish-tomentose and hirsute, slightly shorter than petals; petals yellow, narrowly obovate, rounded (often with a shallow notch), 5-7 mm.
Habitat: Open grassland, sagebrush, juniper scabland, and ponderosa pine forests.
Notes: Native. This species is highly variable in size, color, pubescence, and flower size.
Synonymy: None.

Hitchcock and Cronquist (1977)

Newberry's cinquefoil   *Potentilla newberryi* Gray

Description: Short-lived, prostrate to ascending perennial with a taproot, a simple to branched crown, and leafy stems.

Height: 0.5-3 (5) dm.

Leaves: Mostly cauline, few basal; pinnate, 2-4 cm; leaflets 7-15 (sometimes 5 to 21), pinnately divided into 3-7 linear to elliptic to spatulate segments, each 3-5 (7) mm long.

Pubescence: Grayish-silky to hirsute.

Flowers: Fragrant, generally hidden by foliage; sepals lanceolate 4-5 mm; petals cream or white, obovate, rounded to slightly notched at the apex or obcordate, 5-6 mm; Apr.-July.

Habitat: Dry lake shores, vernal pools, water holes.

Notes: Native. This is an obligate wetland species in this region.

Synonymy: None.

Hitchcock and Cronquist (1977)

Snow cinquefoil   *Potentilla nivea* L.

Description: Short, cushion-like grayish perennial from a branched crown and short rootstocks.

Height: 3-15 cm.

Leaves: Ternate; leaflets oblong-obovate to oval, 5-15 mm; leaflet margins toothed (usually 7-11) about halfway to midvein.

Pubescence: Grayish-tomentose throughout except for greenish, strigose-hirsute upper surface of leaves.

Flowers: Varies from few flowered (1-2) and contracted, to a many-flowered (3-9), open inflorescence; sepals lanceolate (3-4 mm), silky to somewhat tomentose; petals yellow, obcordate, and 1-2 mm longer than sepals; June-Aug.

Habitat: Alpine slopes and meadows.

Notes: Native. This species has variable pubescence, leaf size, flower size, and general growth characteristics.

Synonymy: None.

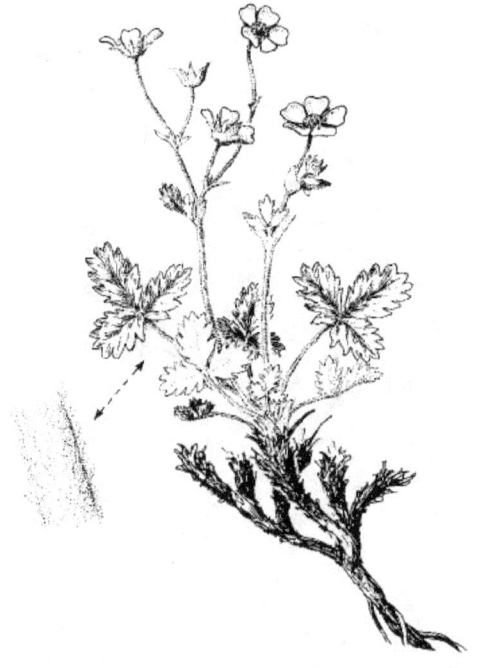

Hitchcock and Cronquist (1977)

34

Norwegian cinquefoil   *Potentilla norvegica* L.

Description: A simple to
  branching, upright annual or
  biennial.
Height: 3-6 (8) dm.
Leaves: Mostly cauline; ternate
  (rarely 5-foliate); leaflets
  broadly ovate to obovate on
  lower plant, to narrowly oblong
  on upper plant, usually 3-6 cm,
  spreading- to appressed-hirsute.
  Margins crenate-serrate.
Pubescence: Strongly hirsute on
  lower plant to subtomentose on
  upper plant; eglandular; large
  hairs often with small pustules
  at the base.
Flowers: Long-pedunculate
  compact cymes. Sepals broadly
  lanceolate, strigose to hirsute,
  eglandular to glandular puberulent. Petals yellow, broadly
  obovate and often notched at
  the apex, from ¾ to as long as
  the sepals; May-Aug.
Habitat: Widespread but
  occasional. Usually on moist
  soils and waste places.
Notes: Questionably native in
  this area.
Synonymy: None.

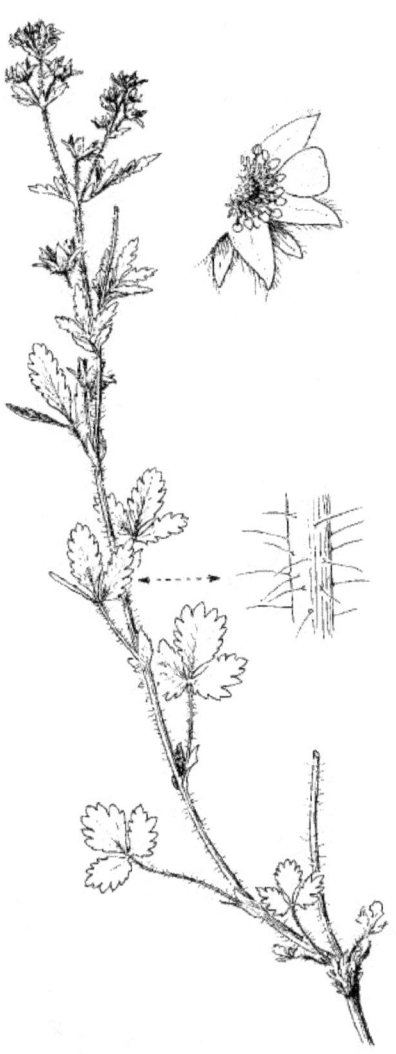

Hitchcock and Cronquist (1977)

Sheep cinquefoil

Potentilla ovina
Macoun ex J.M. Macoun

Description: Spreading to erect, grayish to greenish perennial from strong crown with short, thick rhizomes.

Height: 0.5-1.5 (2.5) dm.

Leaves: Mostly basal; pinnate with short petioles; leaflets usually 9-21, sometimes crowded, 5-12 mm, pedately divided nearly to base into 3-5 (7) linear segments; lower surface of leaves often grayish.

Pubescence: Mostly sericeous-hirsute, occasionally with (irregularly) curled, or crooked hairs.

Flowers: Open, spreading to ascending cymes with 3-7 flowers; sepals acutely to acuminately lanceolate, 3.5-5 mm; petals yellow, obcordate, 1-2 mm longer than the sepals.

Habitat: Moist meadows to open ridges, barren slopes, from montane to alpine zones.

Notes: Native. Hitchcock and Cronquist (1977) note that the species varies considerably in the number and degree of leaflet dissections, as well as general pubescence.

Synonymy: None.

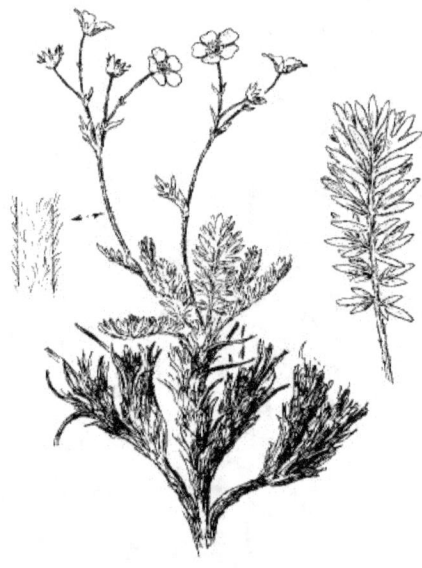

Hitchcock and Cronquist (1977)

Paradox cinquefoil

Potentilla paradoxa Nutt.

Description: Tall, simple or
branched, leafy, taprooted
biennial or short-lived perennial.

Height: 4-7 (9) dm.

Leaves: Pinnate; lower leaves with
2-4 (sometimes 5) pairs of
elliptic to oblong leaflets,
crenate-serrate, 1-3 cm; terminal
leaflets sometimes confluent;
upper leaves sometimes ternate.

Pubescence: Glabrous on lower
plant to strongly hirsute above.

Flowers: Sepals ovate-triangular,
3-4 mm, hirsute; petals yellow,
obovate, and subequal to the
sepals; June-July.

Habitat: Sandy streambanks, lake
shores, moist flats.

Notes: Native. Uncommon in
this region. This is a facultative
wetland species. It is listed as
threatened in Michigan and
Ohio, and as endangered in
New York and Pennsylvania.

Synonymy: *Potentilla nicolletii*
(S. Wats.) Sheldon; *P. supina* L.
ssp. *paradoxa* (Nutt.) Soják.

Hitchcock and Cronquist (1977)

Combleaf cinquefoil

Potentilla pectinisecta Rydb.

Description: Pubescent perennial from a thick, scaly caudex, often branched.

Height: 3-8 dm.

Leaves: Basal, digitate; leaflets 5-9, lanceolate to oblong-elliptic, 2-8 cm; leaflet margins dissected at least ⅔ of the way to midvein into linear or narrowly lanceolate segments; upper surface greenish, lower surface grayish-green sericeous; petioles 5-10 cm.

Pubescence: Appressed to spreading hairy.

Flowers: Open, many-flowered inflorescence; sepals broadly lanceolate, hairy; petals yellow, obcordate, 5-8 mm; June-Aug.

Habitat: Montane; dry to moist meadows, grasslands, rocky slopes, open forests, roadsides, and waste places.

Notes: Native. This species is easily confused with *P. gracilis* var. *flabelliformis,* which has white-tomentose leaf undersurfaces, revolute margins, and long petioles (10-25 cm).

Synonymy: *Potentilla gracilis* Dougl. ex Hook. var. *elmeri* (Rydb.) Jepson.

Modified from Hitchcock and Cronquist (1977)

Pennsylvania cinquefoil   *Potentilla pensylvanica* L.

Description: Decumbent to erect perennial from a branched caudex.
   Height: 2-5 (7) dm.

Leaves: Pinnate; heavily pubescent, upper surface usually greenish, lower
   surface nearly white; leaflets 5-9 (sometimes 11), oblong to oblanceolate,
   1.5-3 cm, the lower ones reduced and the upper 3 largest; each leaflet
   laciniately lobed ½ to ⅔ of the way to the midrib into linear segments
   oriented toward the leaflet tip.

Pubescence: Sparsely to thickly pubescent, usually tomentose.

Flowers: Several-flowered narrow cymes; sepals triangular-lanceolate,
   grayish-strigose-tomentose and more or less glandular, about 5 mm;
   petals yellow and about as long as the sepals; June-Aug.

Habitat: Grasslands, sagebrush plains, montane ridges.

Notes: Native. This species is listed as threatened in Iowa and Michigan.

Synonymy: None.

Hitchcock and Cronquist (1977)

Beautiful cinquefoil

Potentilla pulcherrima **Lehm.**

Description: Pubescent perennial from a thick, scaly caudex, often branched.

Height: 3-8 dm.

Leaves: Basal, digitate; leaflets 5-9, lanceolate to oblong-elliptic, 2-8 cm; leaflet margins evenly toothed ⅓ to ½ of the way to midvein; upper surfaces greenish and spreading hairy, lower surface densely white tomentose.

Pubescence: Appressed to spreading hairy.

Flowers: Open, many-flowered inflorescence; sepals broadly lanceolate, hairy; petals yellow, obcordate, 6-10 mm; June-Aug.

Habitat: Montane; dry to moist meadows, grasslands, rocky slopes, open forests, roadsides, and waste places.

Notes: Native. This species is freely transitional to *P. gracilis* var. *brunnescens* in parts of Wyoming and Montana, where this species also may have minute glandular-pubescence on the leaves and the calyx.

Synonymy: *Potentilla camporum* Rydb.; *P. gracilis* Dougl. ex Hook. var. *pulcherrima* (Lehm.) Fern.

Modified from Hitchcock and Cronquist (1977)

Sulfur cinquefoil   *Potentilla recta* L.

Description: Erect, greenish
  perennial from a simple to
  branched caudex.
Height: 3-8 dm.
Leaves: Mostly cauline and
  oriented upright, digitate;
  leaflets 5-7, oblanceolate,
  prominently veined, 3-8 cm;
  leaflet margins serrate-lobate
  about halfway to midvein, teeth
  divergent and antrose.
Pubescence: Sparsely to copiously
  hirsute to semihispid and with
  more abundant, shorter,
  spreading, sometimes glandular
  pubescence; longer hairs on
  stem usually as long as stem is
  wide; hairs sometimes sparkle
  in full sun.
Flowers: Large, multiflowered
  cymes. Sepals acuminate,
  prominently veined, 5-9 mm;
  petals pale yellow, obovate,
  notched at the apex and up to
  3 mm longer than the sepals;
  June-July.
Habitat: Disturbed areas.
Note: Introduced from Eurasia
  and now a well-established
  ruderal. Similar to *P. argentea*
  in having cauline leaves.
  However, *P. argentea* is typically
  smaller and covered by grayish
  tomentum. This species is
  listed as a noxious weed in
  Colorado, Montana, Wyoming,
  Oregon, and Washington.

Hitchcock and Cronquist (1977)

Synonymy: *Potentilla recta* L.
  var. *obscura* (Nestler) W.D.J.
  Koch; *P. recta* L. var. *pilosa*
  (Willd.) Ledeb.; *P. recta* L. var.
  sulphurea (Lam. & DC.) Peyr.

41

Brook cinquefoil   *Potentilla rivalis* **Nutt.**

Description: Erect, leafy, spreading annual or biennial with a strong
   taproot and usually a simple caudex.
Height: 1-4 (sometimes up to 6) dm.
Leaves: Cauline and basal; 3- to 5-foliate; leaflets oval, up to 4 cm,
   coarsely crenate.
Pubescence: Strongly, finely pubescent, spreading to appressed, often
   almost tomentose.
Flowers: Calyx cup-shaped, 5-10 mm wide; sepals ovate-triangular
   3-4 mm; petals yellow, cuneate-obovate to broadly oblanceolate,
   rounded, 1.3-2.7 mm.; May-Sept.
Habitat: Damp soils, especially in riparian areas, and around lakes
   and ponds.
Note: Native. This species is a facultative wetland species in the Blue
   Mountains region.
Synonymy: None.

var. *millegrana*

var. *rivalis*

Hitchcock and Cronquist (1977)

One-flowered cinquefoil   *Potentilla uniflora* Ledeb.

Description: Hairy, grayish hairy perennial with branched crown and
short root stocks.

Height: 5-15 cm.

Leaves: Ternate; lower surface grayish tomentose, upper surface hirsute
and somewhat greenish; petioles with undulate to nearly straight,
slightly tangled long silky hairs; leaflets cuneate-obovate to obovate-
rhombic, 1-2 cm; leaflet margins dentate-lobate about halfway to
midvein with 7-11 ovate-lanceolate teeth.

Pubescence: Densely and variously hairy throughout.

Flowers: Cymes 1 to 2 (3) flowered; sepals lanceolate, silky to partially
tomentose, 3-4 mm; petals yellow, 4-5 mm; June-July.

Habitat: River bars to alpine ridges and rock crevices.

Note: Native. Can be confused with *P. nivea* and *P. villosa*. However,
P. nivea lacks tomentum on the petioles, and *P. villosa* has wider calyx
bracteoles and larger flowers.

Synonymy: None.

Hitchcock and Cronquist (1977)

43

Villous cinquefoil   *Potentilla villosa*
                                                          Pallas ex Pursh

Description: Densely pubescent, grayish perennial with branched crown
  and short, stout ascending root stocks.

Height: 3-15 cm.

Leaves: Thick, leathery; prominently veined; ternate; leaftlets cuneate-
  obovate to flabelliform, 1-2 cm; leaflet margins coarsely crenate-dentate
  up to ⅓ of the way to the midvein with rounded teeth; usually 2
  cauline leaves.

Pubescence: Grayish-villous or somewhat appressed silky throughout;
  stems, calyx, and lower surfaces of the leaves usually woolly.

Flowers: Open, 2- to 5-flowered cymes; sepals triangular, 3.5-4.5 mm;
  petals yellow, obcordate, usually 5-8 mm; July-Sept.

Habitat: Alpine ridges, talus slopes, and rock crevices.

Note: Native.

Synonymy: *P. nivea* L. var. *villosa* (Pallas ex Pursh) Regel & Tiling.

Hitchcock and Cronquist (1977)

Glossary

annual–A plant that germinates from seed, flowers, sets seed, and dies the same year.

antrorse–Directed forward or upward, for example, toward the leaf or leaflet tip.

biennial–A plant that lives 2 years. Usually the plant forms a basal rosette of leaves during the first year, then flowers, sets seed, and dies in the second year.

calyx–A collective term for all the sepals of a flower.

cauline–Leaves arising from the stem above ground level.

congested–Densely crowded or clustered so that when laid flat the parts overlap.

cordate–Heart shaped with the notch at the point of attachment.

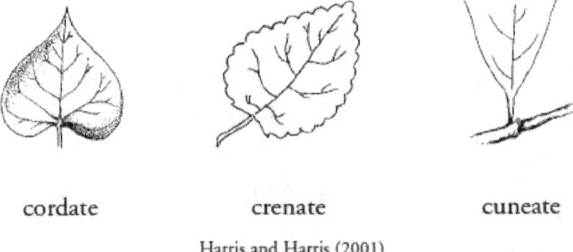

cordate   crenate   cuneate

Harris and Harris (2001)

crenate–With rounded teeth along the margin; scalloped.

cuneate–Triangular or wedge shaped, narrowest end at the point of attachment.

cyme–A flat- or round-topped inflorescence in which the terminal flower blooms first.

digitate–A compound leaf that is lobed or divided from a common point, much like the fingers of a hand.

digitate   glandular

Harris and Harris (2001)

eglandular–Without glands.

facultative wetland species–A U.S. Fish and Wildlife Service designation for a species with a high affinity for wetlands. In other words, if you find a species with this designation, there is a 67- to 99-percent probability that you are in a wetland.

glabrate–Almost glabrous.

glabrous–Smooth, lacking hairs or glands.

glandular–Glandlike; having an appendage, protuberance, or other structure that secretes sticky or oily substances.

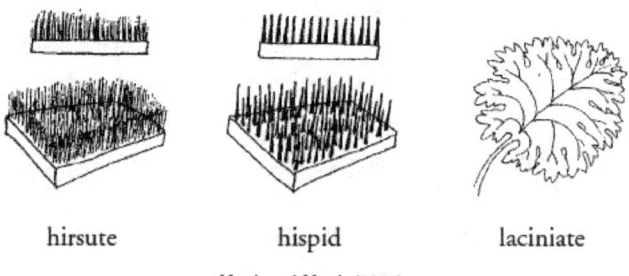

hirsute   hispid   laciniate

Harris and Harris (2001)

glaucous–Covered with a bluish or whitish waxy bloom, such as on the surface of a plum.

hirsute–Pubescent with coarse, stiff, upright hairs.

hispid–Rough with firm, stiff hairs that are bristlelike.

inflorescence–The flowering part of the plant, and also the arrangement of the flowers along the axis.

laciniate–Cut into narrow irregular or unequal lobes or segments.

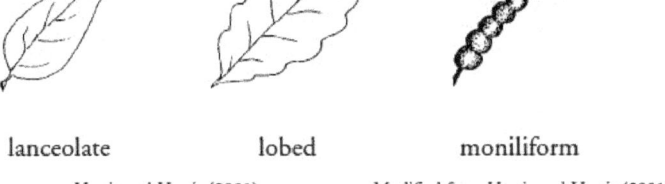

lanceolate   lobed   moniliform

Harris and Harris (2001)   Modified from Harris and Harris (2001)

lanceolate–Lance-shaped; much longer than wide with the widest point below the middle.

lobed–Rounded divisions or segments of the leaf that are cut less than halfway to the midvein.

moniliform–Necklace-like; cylindrical and constricted at regular intervals.

ob–Prefix meaning inversion, or in a reverse direction, such as obovate.

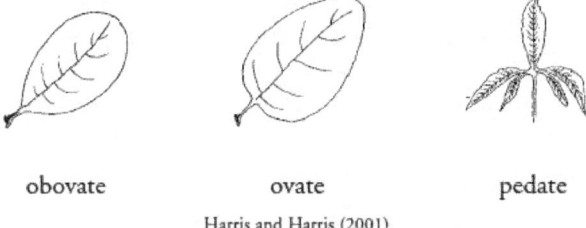

obovate   ovate   pedate

Harris and Harris (2001)

obligate wetland species–A U.S. Fish and Wildlife Service designation for species that almost always occur in natural conditions in wetlands.

ovate–Egg-shaped in two-dimensional outline and attached at the broad end.

pedate–Digitately divided with the lateral two lobes cleft in two.

perennial–A plant that lives at least 3 years.

petiole–The leaf stalk; connects the blade to the stem.

pilose–Having long, soft, straight hairs.

pilose

Harris and Harris (2001)

pinnate–In a compound leaf, the leaflets are arranged on opposite sides of an elongated main axis.

  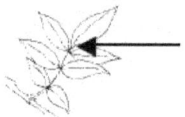

pinnate   puberulent   rachis

Harris and Harris (2001)   Modified from Harris and Harris (2001)

puberulent–Minutely pubescent with fine short hairs.

pubescent–Having hairs of any sort.

rachis–The central axis of a compound leaf.

revolute–Having margins that are rolled back toward the underside of the leaf.

rhizome–A long, horizontal stem growing below ground, generally rootlike in appearance.

ruderal–Weedy; growing in disturbed habitats or waste places.

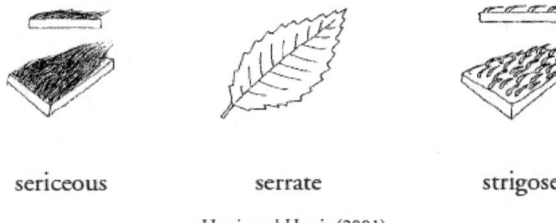

sericeous   serrate   strigose

Harris and Harris (2001)

sericeous–Silky with long soft somewhat flattened hairs.

serrate–Sawlike; toothed along the margin, with the teeth pointing forward.

stolon–A long, horizontal stem growing above ground, forming roots at the nodes or tip and thus producing new plants.

strigose–Having straight, stiff, sharp hairs oriented parallel to the surface.

sub–Prefix meaning "not quite."

ternate   tomentose

Harris and Harris (2001)

ternate–Divided into threes, such as a strawberry leaf.

tomentose–Covered with short, matted or tangled, soft woolly hairs.

villous–Bearing long, soft, shaggy hairs that are unmatted.

woolly–Densely covered with long, tangled hairs.

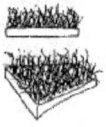

villous

woolly

Harris and Harris (2001)

Modified from Harris and Harris (2001)